My State MICHIGAN

By Christina Earley

TABLE OF CONTENTS

A Crabtree Seedlings Book

Crabtree Publishing

crabtreebooks.com

School-to-Home Support for Caregivers and Teachers

This book helps children grow by letting them practice reading. Here are a few guiding questions to help the reader build his or her comprehension skills. Possible answers appear in red.

Before Reading:

- What do I know about Michigan?
  - *I know that Michigan is a state.*
  - *I know that Michigan is surrounded by four of the Great Lakes.*

- What do I want to learn about Michigan?
  - *I want to learn which famous people were born in Michigan.*
  - *I want to learn what the state flag looks like.*

During Reading:

- What have I learned so far?
  - *I have learned that Lansing is the state capital of Michigan.*
  - *I have learned that some of the cliffs at Pictured Rocks National Lakeshore are 200 feet (60 m) high.*
- I wonder why...
  - *I wonder why the state flower is the apple blossom.*
  - *I wonder why Mackinac Island is known for its fudge.*

After Reading:

- What did I learn about Michigan?
  - *I have learned that there are many sea animals at SEA LIFE Michigan.*
  - *I have learned that the state animal is the white-tailed deer.*

- Read the book again and look for the glossary words.
  - *I see the word **capital** on page 6, and the word **factory** on page 17. The other glossary words are found on pages 22 and 23.*

MICHIGAN
Hi! My name is Bailey. Welcome to Michigan!

I live on Mackinac Island. There are many **historic** buildings here.

Mackinac Island is known for its world-famous fudge!

Michigan is in the **midwestern** United States. The **capital** is Lansing.

Fun Fact: Detroit is the largest city in Michigan.

The state animal is the white-tailed deer.

The apple blossom is the state flower.

We grow a lot of blueberries in Michigan. Some of them are used to make blueberry muffins.

Fun Fact: About 100 million pounds (45 million kg) of blueberries are grown in Michigan each year.

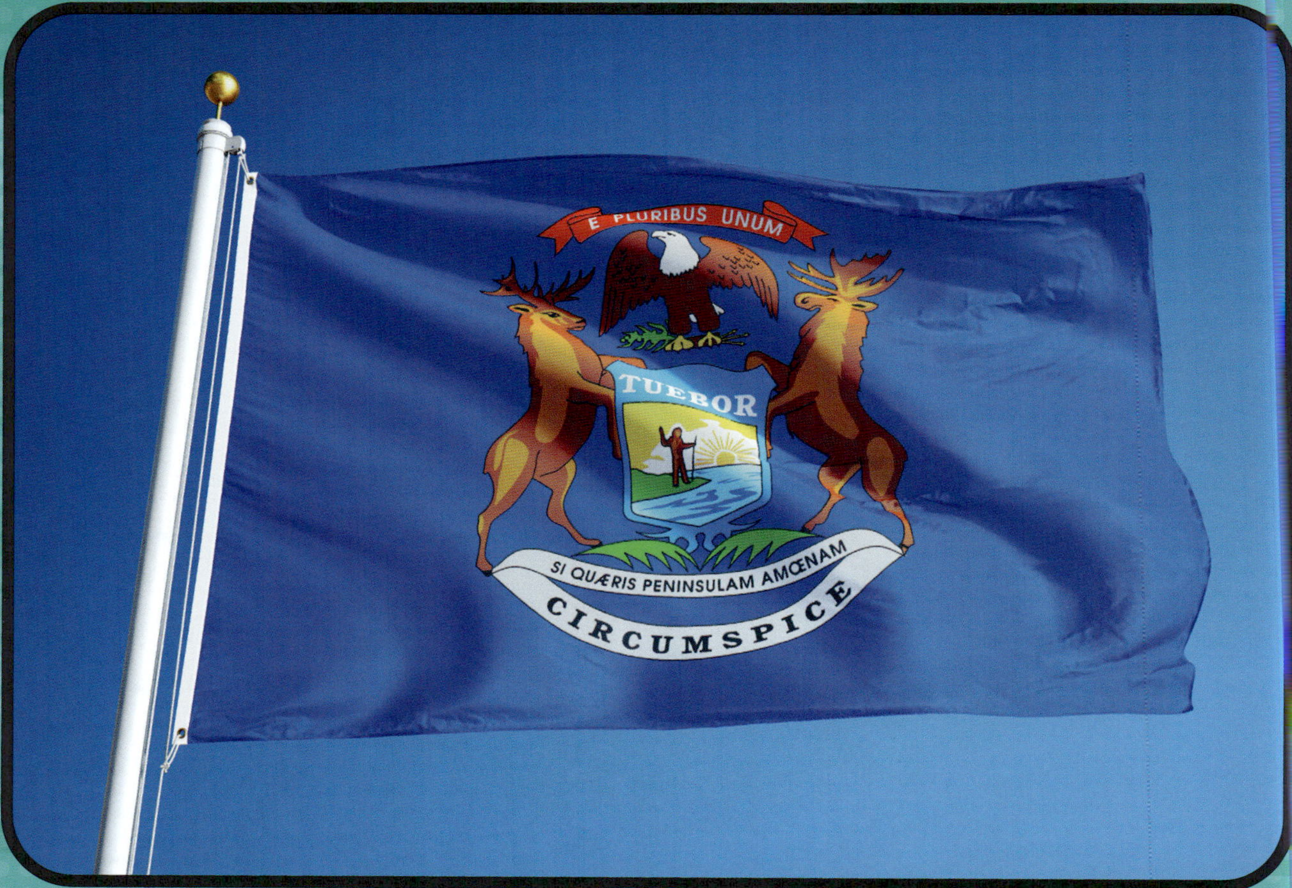

My state flag is blue. The state **coat of arms** is in the middle.

There are four national sports teams in Michigan.

Pictured Rocks National Lakeshore has sandstone cliffs. Chapel Rock is my favorite.

Fun Fact: Some of the cliffs are 200 feet (60 m) high.

I enjoy fishing for trout on Lake Superior.

I can take a tour of the Ford Rouge **Factory** to learn how a car is made.

Singer Madonna was born in Michigan. Tennis **legend** Serena Williams was also born in Michigan.

Fun Fact: President Gerald R. Ford grew up in Grand Rapids, Michigan.

Dogsledding on Sugarloaf Mountain is fun.

There are lots of sea animals to see at SEA LIFE Michigan aquarium.

Glossary

capital (cap-ih-tuhl): The city or town where the government of a country, state, or province is located

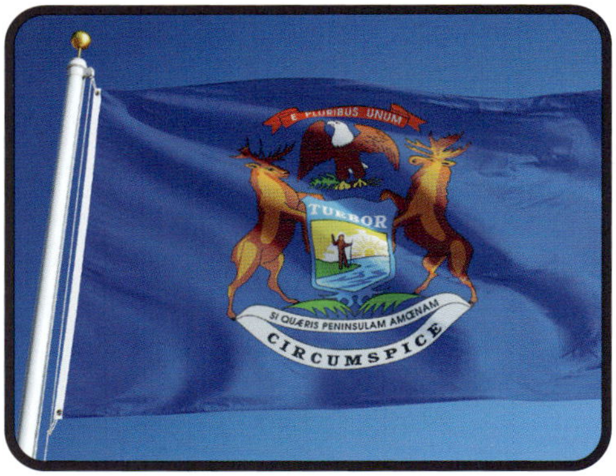

coat of arms (coht uv armz): A special group of pictures, usually shown on a shield

factory (fak-tor-ee): A building where machines are used to make things

historic (hi-stor-ik): Something that is important in history

legend (leh-jind): A very famous person who is known for doing something well

midwestern (mid-west-urn): The northern central part of the United States

Index

About the Author

Christina Earley lives in sunny South Florida with her husband and son. She enjoys traveling around the United States and learning about different historical places. Her hobbies include hiking, yoga, and baking.

Written by: Christina Earley
Designed and Illustrated by: Bobbie Houser
Series Development: James Earley
Proofreader: Melissa Boyce
Educational Consultant: Marie Lemke M.Ed.

Photographs:
Shutterstock: Travis J. Camp: cover; ehrlif: p. 3; Craig Sterken: p. 4, 23; gg5795: p. 5; Volina: p. 6, 22-23; Andrey Bayda: p. 7; Tom Reichner: p. 8; Natali Glado: p. 9; Bryan Pollard: p. 10-11; Krasula: p. 11; railway fx: p. 12, 22; Steve Sykes: p. 13; John McCormick: p. 14-15; Wildnerdpix: p. 15; Craig Sterken: p. 16; JHVEPhoto: p. 17, 22; Denis Makarenko: p. 18 left; Tinseltown: p. 18 right, 23; COLOMBO NICOLA: p. 20; BlackFarm: p. 21
whitehouse.gov: p. 19

Crabtree Publishing

crabtreebooks.com 800-387-7650

Printed in the U.S.A./072023/CG20230214

Published in Canada
Crabtree Publishing
616 Welland Avenue
St. Catharines, Ontario
L2M 5V6

Published in the United States
Crabtree Publishing
347 Fifth Avenue
Suite 1402-145
New York, New York, 10016

Library and Archives Canada Cataloguing in Publication
Available at Library and Archives Canada

Library of Congress Cataloging-in-Publication Data
Available at the Library of Congress

Hardcover: 978-1-0398-0545-3
Paperback: 978-1-0398-0577-4
Ebook (pdf): 978-1-0398-0641-2
Epub: 978-1-0398-0609-2